Artist by Night

ABEL CORNEJO

Copyright © 2016 Abel Cornejo

Cover illustration by Nicole Cousino

All rights reserved.

ISBN: **0692638024**
ISBN-13: **978-0692638026**

DEDICATION

A cross-complication of work spanning 20 years of
interdisciplinary exploration and theatre-making.

To all artists who work by day,
to pursue their passion at night.

CONTENTS

Acknowledgments	i
Plaster and Flesh	3
You're Different	22
Wilton Place	23
Suspicious Activity	30
Sabanas	36
Miami Monologs	37
COLLIDE	38
UTOPIA D2H	40

ACKNOWLEDGMENTS

Many thanks to the artists and influences that have added color to my life. Nicole Cousino, Sarah Lewison, Agathea Pappas, Pina Sbrocca, Jean Minuchin, Helen Reynolds, David Pearson, Johann Abreu, Dominick Daniel, Blaze Powers, Andrew Obeidy, World and Eye Arts Center, Miami Light Project, Beth Boone, Rebekah Lengel, Sevim Abaza, Lourdes Cornejo-Krohn

I hide them behind my clichéd fists
Tears
More than just one…many….oh so many

My eyes spout with salty rivers which
run over the hills of my cheeks
through the valleys of my neck
and over the bed of my heart

Say not, feel not they said
But what pain grasps me at the bowels?

Loneliness

Not a friend, not a sister, not even a soul brother

I scream and I kick
I yell and I pull
I write and I type

Maybe…someday I'll stop crying
When? I do not know
For now, I'm sad
So really, really sad

Will anyone wipe my tears?

I had to leave Paris. I left Paris. With crumbles of bagels still fresh on my collar.

I had to leave to see the Golden Gate Bridge. I had to leave her still waiting for soap. Where is the soap?

I took a plane, it started to rain.
Did I remember all of my stuff?
Could I dissolve the two of us? Would I ride a Dodge to work? Could I ride a Dodge to work?

Boy this coat really stinks.
Inks, finks and French pinks.
Then I found a paper in my pocket.
A letter from the one still waiting for the soap.

"You no lika me
I no lika you
We no lika we
So signed and written Maire"

I took my mitten, that worn-torn bitten thing of a mitten and swallowed it.
I ate and I ate. Then eight and eight.
Seven less passengers. Six more pounds…..

Five fingers I licked after munching down the Basset hounds.

But I could not eat the soap. The soap that she was still waiting for.
I washed my face and I scrubbed behind my ears

Using the water from my tears. The salty water burned my skin.
I scratched the lather off with my fingernails.

Then climbed out of the swimming pool and carved a replica of the Golden Gate Bridge with the bar of soap,
that she was still waiting for.

The Catalyst

I would give anything to be your lover,
to touch your Aloe-Vera conditioned skin
to hug you with my boney arms
Woman
can I buy you out?
Roses, Wonder bread
a can of refried beans
I'll let you use my stereo
wash my underwear
and pull grey hair from my head
Are you easy?
Adventuresome
Hungry for some real Latin love
My organs are yours, forever
Wet or naked
Take it, take it
You need a good stinking smell of a man
in your bed
Don't lie to yourself, honey
Look at these lips
And whisper…………
my name, over and over
I adore you but you do not realize it
I am not lint
I deserve more than just tumble and
bye.

The Neutralizer

She rather forget about the one
who gave her all his energy
He, what a pitiful pile of bones
He writes and weeps
Hoping that she will remember
The clinging embraces of dependency
What a balloon! What a tortilla!
A fragile, light, passionate relationship
with this Hispanic he
An emotionally unstable man

(To be read with a fake French accent)

Samwa faire, samwa faire
Samwa faire is everywhere
And everything you see and do
Samwa faire will be there too
And if you try to catch the bus
And you try to hide from us
CIA
FBI
We found you
and know you're through

When I wake
my head I shake
then I call for mommy

Mommy! Mommy!
I want some salami

Then I dress in my school best
and put away my jammies

Jammies! Jammies!

Orange juice,
Beans and
Cheese
God bless these boney knees

Books, bells
I'm swell
Cute poems always sell

Oak and Steiner
Fell and Haight
Drove too fast
Brake, skid, skid
Mam excuse my driving
Grove and damn her
Why and love her
Smell and kiss her
Downshift
Stop sign
Slippery thighs
Danger
What's the cross-street?
Anger
Immaturity
Stupid asshole
Didn't you see the sign
Caution / curves ahead

Stop. Stop. Stop.
Hand over hand
Hand over hand
Left turn
Lean over
Cleavage
Tunnel
Dark and warm
Shouting
Hello, hello
Bouncing all over…..

Pay the toll
Kiss me, kiss me
She chomped on my wrist
Razoring my veins
Coughing up the blood she attempted to suck
A broken 7-up bottle
Front left tire explodes
Back right wheel skids out
Cement column comes forward
Dizzy
Blood drained
Shift
Slam
Roadkill

Five farmers farted
Four fowl flew
Three dogs died
Now spell you
I am me
You are you
Find a dick
and take a pee

Discover the weapon of vision
Unsnarl the blemish of deception
Then disrobe the world of
its havoc
And dissect falsehood, deformity
and distress
Who can stand naked to truth?
I've tried
Hideous, disgusting hair
Haggard disfigured body
Foul dingy smell
Ghostlike
Deathlike
Unliked

I don't care what mother drank
I don't care who father spanks
Cause I hate them anyway
And I'm gonna runaway
Like really far away

PORQUE TU

Y porque tu
y nunca yo?
El suffremento
Los Dolores
El "R" romantico
El "S" stupido
no hay tortillas!
The peacocks in el plaza
The false eyelashes fall
and the birds go to eat them
Your miniskirt is too high
and my ego is too low
Frustrated, angry
The sizzle of Pepsi
the lard in beans
Yucki, fuchci…..I, I, I,
Porque tu y nunca yo

When all lower mid-sections hurt
You might try Quaker oats
or fiber
But chronic muscular disorders
are not carcinogenic
or unhygienic
Rather they, those discomforts
or so to say,
in mother's words,
neurotic transfer of energy,
are unescapable, self-induced
Diseases.
Tongue pressed firmly against the roof of
the mouth.
Curled feet
Tendencies to hold objects too tightly
The grey hair can be dyed
The neck can be massaged
but the mind cannot be lied to.
Altered with drugs
Yes
Oh so many to choose from
Ricky Ran, Ricky Ran
Tic-tic, on and on
I talk to myself
Whole hella-a lot

Hail Mary, Sacramento
Sacred won-ton
Floating piece of meat
Blessed now you…..

I go back
Four, five, six
Spit.
Spit.
Rudimentary of all fixations are
illusionary repressions.

Of this earth I eat
Tomatoes, potatoes and leeks
In water I wash
Good things
green, gold and squash
Orchards of oranges
and rows of radishes
Droplets of water on
tender leaves
Flowers and blossoms
swarming with bees
The sun, the soil
And us all destroying

The Lost Page

mood was set. I ran to her, she ran to me and we embraced when we met. She then asked if I wanted to take a bath in fresh, warm cow's milk.
"I rather drink it," I told her.
"Bath in it," insisted Ms. Zsa Zsa Gabor. In disgust, I turned away while tiny droplets of warm tears formed in my eyes. Before I could take a step, she grabbed my arm, jerked me around and looked deeply into my innocent brown eyes.
"You think you are a goody-goody. Well Mr. 'I'm too good for those games, think about this, you bath in water and you also drink it."
I could take no more. I ran as fast as my Kmart all-stars could take me. In shock, in pain, in tears, in confusion, in disappointment….I did run.

By Request

Love and Sex

Hand and Hand

Wrapped with wiennies

sperm and spam

Gifts and Grunts

I'm on top

Your hair's a mess

Baby you know I'm the best!

Sleeping Pill

Why do men write such things?
Poems, Manifestos
Books and
Lies.
Think back, when all was black
Could you see a pen?
Or a hand to write with?
Swim back further
murky mind
Can you find a reader
a publisher
or a go-go dancer?
Reach behind the dimness
Dark and drowse
Hide beneath the warmth
Doze heavy eyes
Sleep
Nap
Rest
For the insomniacs are awake and
writing.

WRITINGS

From *You're Different: the newsletter for the utmost regard for fingers and friendly igloos*

You're different
You think different
You comb you hair different
You're counter-culture
You're underground
You're not part of any trend
You only wear this.
You never wear that.
You never would think that way
You would never act that way
You're different

From Wilton Place
Los Angeles

Fame brought famine to the house of feasting.
No menu was given to us as we took our seats with bloated tongues.
"You talk too much," said our waiter.
"I never said a word," I righteously responded.
Then the chandelier from above started swinging and dust balls formed from all the grease in the air and started bombing our soft heads(full of righteousness).
"Could this be an earthquake," I asked my fellow intellectual mates.
"Well, this is the month of May," responded the one being the scientist.
"The month of the communist," surly stated the waiter.
"The end of spring," added another.
Then the water pipe from within exploded and water gushed upon our starch-ironed shirts.
"Don't tell me your deceit, your nostril glorification," I yelled as passion overtook me.
"I know more than you do."

From *Wilton Place*

not. said. what missed. sit. memories.
pretty. pretty dress. wait. dreaming. in
my head. back. deep. dark. hands
wrinkled. things touched. plants grow.
water. water. quiet. comb. resting. rug.
sad. posture. click. tap. footsteps.
whisper. sleep.

When all of none
Show up nowhere
Go ahead and stop

From *Wilton Place*

Parkinson's disease is killing
my brother-in-law who had an
affair with my best friend's sister.
My mother left to Texas to visit my
stepfather's mother who also happens
to be my best friend's aunt.
When my cousin phoned to tell me
that my ex-boyfriend was getting
together with my best friend's next-door
neighbor, I had to drive
over to my best friend's house which
happened to be once owned by my
grandmother's great-grandfather.

Parkinson's disease has flown to Texas
and Dallas is my best friend's name.

From *Wilton Place*

Guilt.
You are. Can never. Will always have.
Guilt.
You run from. You confess to.
But never admit to.
Guilt.
Don't' ever. Say never.
You are. And will be. Guilty

From *Wilton Place*

Do you ever find yourself wanting to
write but you can't?
Do you ever find yourself wanting to read
but you can't?
When the can't-s become ants
and they work their way into your head
You'll mingle and tingle
and slowly go to bed with heavy
d's and diseases
Infected with an "i"
"I can't", "I can't", "I can't"

From *Wilton Place*

The little toad girl was always able to suck her own feet. All of the other children were disgusted by this compulsive self-satisfying behavior. Yes her toes were always wrinkly from the hours of bathing in her own saliva. Medical attention was prescribed. What was wrong was not the need to suck, but rather as the doctor said, "Such deviant pubescent behavior of orally and auto promiscuously sucking of one's externals is an unhealthy and vile act of mockery masturbation." He then stuck his finger deep in his ear cleaning out the wax. The little toad girl did not understand. Later, her feet were removed.

THEATRICAL WONDERS

From *Suspicious Activity*, Here and Now Festival, Miami Light Project

I am a criminal and I am an artist
My crime is art
My punishment is this performance.

The infamous Carmina Burana score by Carl Orff was inspired by 24 songs and poems by students and vagrants living in a 12th century monastery in Germany. The writings deal mostly with repressive medieval norms, sex and drinking and banned artistic expression.

It was shortly after September 11 and the attacks on the World Trade Center. And I was working at a theatre and it was opening night and everything was still very tense. People were still apprehensive but it was opening night and we were all looking forward to it. We were opening up the building and then this creepy cop shows up. And he starts locking the doors to the building and I'm like, "What are you doing? People have to come in and use the restroom and see the show." And he's like, "No, no, no, we have to secure the building. I'm like whatever, "But how are people going to get in?" He's like, "They need to take the long way" So I go back to the box office and he stands right in front and starts talking in his little walkie talkie............

in codes "we have a 1329, 4290, blah, blah, blah……..we have some suspicious activity." Suspicious activity? This is theatre. This is people gathering together to see a performance expressing emotions and ideas. Then I'm like "Oh I get it." It's not that the same things happen in history over and over again. But we react by suspecting the same people.

Everything you say and do will be used against you
and anything you <u>don't</u> say and do will be used against you too.

From *Suspicious Activity*, Here and Now Festival, Miami Light Project

Subway

Someday this will all make sense to you
Someday all these words and ramblings which seem so child-like
will rise to the top of the ocean.

Then somebody said,
"Wake up you're at the end of the line."
I was sleeping.
I missed my stop. My stop. What time is it?
Someone said something. My wallet.
My wallet was gone.
They stole my wallet while I was asleep.
They took my credit cards.
Where is the switch? The room was dark so I felt the walls searching for the switch.
Fuck. I stepped on a broken plate.
I didn't want to eat dinner. I didn't want to talk or pretend my life was important so they locked me up in a subway car until I could find myself.
But I missed my chance. I missed my stop.

From *Suspicious Activity*, Here and Now Festival, Miami Light Project

If I asked you…..

If I bought you paper will you write me?
If I sent you colored pencils will you draw me?
If I think of funny things and tell you about my horrible addiction to extreme life experiences will you plagiarize my life and take my name and change it. Fictionalize and distort my pain. Glamorize those who have tormented my soul. Dehumanize the events into cute comedies starring harlots with names like Jennifer Love Hewitt and Ashley Judd. If I ask you to lie for me would you?

From *Suspicious Activity*, Here and Now
Festival, Miami Light Project

Copenhagen, 1352

In this rage and bitterness I talk to myself
If a wise man builds a house high in the
Hollywood Hills
What am I? A fool.
No, I am a big red maple leaf
Floating down the river like a paper boat
through the bubbly waters
searching for others like myself.
I hook up with the mentally deprived
The freaks, the whores, the poets
and the playwrights.

From *Suspicious Activity*, Here and Now
Festival, Miami Light Project

Miami, 1989

So what are you really trying to say!
Fuck the palm trees?
Send everyone back from where they came from?
Spend the rest of my life in a monastery?
Fuck that shit!
Look at all the chaos around us
Now Overtown is on fire.
They're turning over cars, setting everything to flames,
Throwing concrete blocks through windows,
Pulling people out of their cars
One by one sent to Jackson Memorial Hospital
Street after street is destroyed
Overtown is on fire again.
For a third time this decade.
And the newspaper man asks,
How can they burn their own community?
How can someone set themselves afire.

From *Sabanas: Life through Dreams*, New York International Fringe Festival

Charlotte. Something strange has happened. The Xerox machine is following me around. I'm scared for my life. It started Xeroxing strange cosmic star patterns like it was trying to tell me my future. Now it's following me around. Oh my. It's not my fault. Blame the people who put wheels on it.

From *The Miami Monologues*, San Antonio Teatrofest, Guadalupe Cultural Center

Olga Fuentes Garcia:
I am Latina and I cannot be silent.
My words are evocative pictures and the spirits of courageous women ignite my tongue.
Dicen que soy dramatica. Pero vayanse al enferno! Who else will light the fires in this boring dry world.
This illusion we call Miami.
Con las calles de pastelitos. Y casas color de Guayba. Y tiendas de Mango y Mansiones de limas
Las ramas de I95, dolphin expressway y Palmetto freeway extending throughout the garden of paradise
While the trees and waves root into my soul.
Eating, breathing, feeding my hunger for a life filled with exclamations.
And how dare they question.
"Why do women do that to themselves?"
Because we are goddesses
Mystic inspiration
Fruitas de arte que nunca se comen
La tentación de Adán

From *COLLIDE*, World and Eye Arts Center

SKYLAB

Diana:
I've spent my life trying to prove others that I love them. But they never recognized my love.
I hid most of my life from those that actually wanted to help me.
I ate from someone else's plate.
I lived in someone else's house.
I slept in someone else's bed.
Defined by my relationship to that person.
Who never hear me, but heard his voice through me.
I took the direction of what to do and what to say, the script of my life written by this other.

I want you far away from me,
in another universe.
Faint....distant....insignificant.
Get the fuck out of my life!

From *COLLIDE*, World and Eye Arts Center

On a quest for who we are
Exploring though space / time
Who / what
Why / live
Exploding emotional planets
Colliding narcissist asteroids
Resisting conversations with our fears
With one another
Finding fault, forcing face
Faking feelings, falling apart
Fear of intimacy, fear of losing control, fear of change
Fear of failure
Of a marriage collapsing into divorce….distrust
Disfigured hideous meteorite
Violently thrown across the universe
Propelled by anger and disgust…
In you, in me, in what this
whole mess has become
Exploding galaxy in the dark sky
In storm over night
In clouds over secrets
Now whispering, glimmering,
The last moments of existence
A new beginning comes to me.
A cosmic re-generation.

From *UTOPIA D2H*, Here and Now Festival, Miami Light Project

Last Attempt

Hovering in airplane without a pilot
The buzz of the engine is constant
and it won't let me sleep.
The night is vast and endless
But I need to find this other place.
This is my last attempt to find a place called Purpose
The vessel is quiet….. and there's no one on this plane but myself.

Outside the sky's a twinkle with billions of stars around me.
Talking….chatting…. in circles with their closest friends
I feel disconnected…. in a separate dimension.

Detached from the moment I think.
A mental picture takes me away from this social situation.

I wanted life but got an empty box
I wanted red, but got one yellow and two blue
I wanted the aisle seat but got stuck in the middle.

So can I ask you a question? Is it time yet?
When are you going to let people know….

Hunched over / head over food tray
Trying to sleep through this flight
I toss to the left. I toss to the right.
curled up in a fetal position
In my deep sleep, I forget who I am, and everything I wanted to be
I'm ready to die….if this plane goes down.
Row 27, Seat B

From *UTOPIA D2H*, Here and Now Festival, Miami Light Project

<u>YOU</u>
You- You established this distrust of other people with more money than you
You – You failed the American dream
You- You take more from the world than you're willing to give.
You- You lost hope
Wow- You still expect me to talk to you.
Hey, it's time to experiment with possible new models of collective life
As a public, as a one-ness
Catalyze greater connectivity with our inhabitants
Seek other ways to transform cities
Gone are the customary systems
Give rise to revitalizing places for social exchange and public use
Urban gardens and collective meals, with open-air kitchens and cinemas in the square
Free schools and bike trails built upon abandon lands
Designing street furnishings with second hand materials
Occupy it, use it,
Eating meals together, resting together, talking to other people.
A vision of a utopia….
Rudely interrupted with the coughing and sneezing on my back
The friendly skies turn contagious……

Frightened by phobias and distrust
Too intimate, too neighborly, you know too much of my business
Distance creates safety
Starbucks creates lattes
Selfies on cellphones cloud the community
It's "look at me," instead of, "look at us."

From *UTOPIA D2H*, Here and Now Festival, Miami Light Project

DESIRE TO HOME > D2H

The desire to home

The impulse to shelter

The need to furnish

An unexplained pattern of nesting
A phenomenon of social co-habitation.

The desire to home, D2H is chemical compound found in our blood.

Genetically modified human desires or GMHd's are produced from organisms that have had specific changes introduced into their DNA using the methods of genetic engineering.

To live together

To bound together

To reside in community

D2H is in our DNA.

From *UTOPIA D2H*, Here and Now Festival, Miami Light Project

The Waiting Room

The waiting room is for waiting.
One hour is really two and a half

Next hour is really,7 hours later
"Your next," is really
"I don't care about you, just get out of my face."

"Sit over there," means "give us a chance to
talk about you behind your back"

"We're sorry" is really, "We're going to google
your name then charge you double."

The waiting room is for waiting

No activities, no swimming pool
No tennis courts, no tread mills,
just chairs.
All facing the same direction

What about arranging them chaotic all about
the place? Some up, some down, some used
to create tepees.

All equally spaced apart. All identical.
In the waiting room,
you know no one in a land of no where.

From *UTOPIA D2H*, Here and Now Festival,
Miami Light Project

AFLOAT

Reaching for the top, water filling nostrils

Fish against skin,
Sand tugging toes

Gasping to get out,
Gasping to get move up.

Waves crashing against ears
louder than thoughts
confusing the way out.

Summer moon shifts flow

Don't be afraid of your choices

Teacher by day. Artist by night

It seemed like a plan I thought up so many years ago.
But I've changed and the plan remained the same. ….

Broken seaweed litters shore, unhinged from paradise reef

There's a point in your life when you have to change.

This is not working

Reaching for the top,
kicking off expectations

I can't live like this anymore

Reaching further,
pounding harder,
fighting further.

From *UTOPIA D2H*, Here and Now Festival, Miami Light Project

Riding it Out

I've been married now for 7 years. Riding it out, waiting for it to become the dream they all talk about.

Hey, you don't think I know what you're saying about me. Fuck off.

You know I'm tired of this shit. And all this attitude.

Why am I doing this? There has to be a bigger reason.

26 hundred men building a wall to stop the hurricane, there is no reason for staying.

Destruction at 105 miles per hour is on its way.

Why do people even try?

From *UTOPIA D2H*, Here and Now Festival, Miami Light Project

ON A NEW HIGHWAY

On the highway to positive attitude
Get your shit together, gleaming light of enlightenment
Dusty boots, mud covered cynicism
…..washed away.
Wind-ripping futurist outlook
Bio-degradable relationship
What once was, now re-purposed
Building structures from waste
Utilizing old gigabits of memory, of bad experiences, to construct new data
Understanding complex eco-systems of big ego eating supportive artistic type
Transforming false fears to mechanisms of human desires
You can rewrite memories. You can create love. You can erase the hate
Transcend the negative impulse
and re-wire your life.

End Notes

Plaster and Flesh was written while working at the San Francisco Public Library and running the Armpit Gallery, a performance and visual arts space located at 633 Haight Street. It was originally distributed by City Lights Bookstore as a zine. Nicole Cousino and Sarah Lewison were co-curators of the Armpit Gallery and collaborators in numerous artistic projects. *Wilton Place* is an unpublished manuscript mostly written while living in Los Angeles right after the LA riots. *Suspicious Activity* was commissioned by Miami Light Project for the Here and Now Festival: 2002. I created the work in response to the numerous articles about professors and artists being heavily surveillance after 911. Several years later, while teaching at Broward College I wrote and produced *Collide*. The play was performed at the World and Eye Arts Center. Shortly thereafter I was commissioned for the second time by the Miami Light Project to create a new work entitled *Utopia:D2H* for the Here and Now Festival 2014. My work often explores the themes of searching for meaning and belonging and the struggle between the ideal world vs. reality.

With one foot on the ground and the other in the air,
Abel Cornejo
abelart707@gmail.com

www.ingramcontent.com/pod-product-compliance
Lightning Source LLC
Chambersburg PA
CBHW061256040426
42444CB00010B/2394